THINKING OUTSIDE THE BLOCK

AHMAD ABDULLAH

Copyright © 2021 by Ahmad Abdullah.

All rights reserved. No part of this book may be reproduced in any form or by any electronic or mechanical means, including information storage and retrieval systems, without permission in writing from the publisher, except by reviewers, who may quote brief passages in a review.

This publication contains the opinions and ideas of its author. It is intended to provide helpful and informative material on the subjects addressed in the publication. The author and publisher specifically disclaim all responsibility for any liability, loss, or risk, personal or otherwise, which is incurred as a consequence, directly or indirectly, of the use and application of any of the contents of this book.

WRITERS REPUBLIC L.L.C.
515 Summit Ave. Unit R1
Union City, NJ 07087, USA

Website: *www.writersrepublic.com*
Hotline: *1-877-656-6838*
Email: *info@writersrepublic.com*

Ordering Information:
Quantity sales. Special discounts are available on quantity purchases by corporations, associations, and others. For details, contact the publisher at the address above.

Library of Congress Control Number:	2020953025
ISBN-13: 978-1-63728-109-3	[Paperback Edition]
978-1-63728-110-9	[Digital Edition]

Rev. date: 02/10/2021

IN THE NAME OF ALLAH, May Allah be pleased
with all the believing men and women. Amen.

    I would like to dedicate this book to all the brothers and sisters I've lost along the way starting with the way Morroccos spreading my love across the track to the1500 and beyond 16 th&Wyo famly too there's far too many names to mention unfortunately I could find photos for everyone but those who know me and know those I've lost and love know it goes out to them too. We gotta stop killing each other y'all!!!! This can't be stressed enough but any difference this appeal can make I pray it can. I was waiting for photos from a brother who doing LIFE of him and some other homies doing them letters but it was taking longer than I wanted to wait. This goes out to them too and those I don't know doing the same. I can't forget to acknowledge and support those putting forth all their efforts to remain upright be examples of good for their families and communities I salute you not enough attention is given to y'all I love you for the good you do I look forward to the day the good prevails over the bad in being highlighted as it is rightfully so needed and truthfully speaking it is more dominant than advertised.

Prelude, by Daniel Johnson

On a dark ,rainy ,cold night at Jefferson hospital in center city Philadelphia, a young African American mother gave birth to two healthy twin boys named Jay & Ray Brown ,The beautiful strong single mother name Kay Brown abandoned by the father when he learned of the pregnancy ,needless to say it was a struggle for the new mom buy she loved her boys an was very happy they were born ……., The fact her boys were beginning there life journey under the same circumstances it was evident early on that the boys had very different outlooks and ways of thinking about their poverty stricken way of living ,dangerous and very humble household and neighborhood ,not having the presence of a father along with the struggles of growing up as a young black youth In America and the unforgiving inner-city of north philly …….whats the phrase ? cup half empty cup half full , that was the brothers so-to-speak Ray was the traditional pessimist he viewed there life with their mother having to work two dead end jobs and still barely making ends meet ,having to navigate through drug pushers ,pimps ,junkies, prostitutes, gang banners etc. just to get to school and not having that guide ,motivational male figure to help keep their chin up wore heavy on Ray he had a negative way at looking at every situation and would often lash out getting into fights at school and the neighborhood and just displaying anger resentment and other negative emotions that would constantly have him in unwanted an sometimes dangerous situations that kept him in trouble whereas his brother Jay had a more optimistic way at looking at things as it pertained to their lives as he learned by just having a more positive perspective was very beneficial to him in his day-to-day, for example the things that would frustrate & overwhelm Ray , Jay would embrace as just another life challenge or obstacle ,that he would have to overcome to reach his goals ,When momma Kay would struggle with bills and household finances, Jay took that as motivation to work harder in school to educate himself and also get after school jobs to assist his Mom Ray t would let every issue anger him and his negative emotions always took him down the wrong path of committing criminal offenses to earn illegal , income that would intern put him and his family in an even more difficult position . So that's why our Author Shelve Carter-Ahmad Abdullah recognizes the need for this book. He fully understands the self-esteem and drive that being optimistic ,positive and open mindedness provides ,and his experiences & qualifications makes him the perfect man to address these subjects and generational issues ,in particular our youth , he encourages our youth that not only positive vibes are essential to your success ,equally important is something as simple as your language is a great place to start .The way you express yourself and the words you use are a direct reflection of who you are, as well as who you inspire to be , our movement focuses on reprogramming & rewiring our brains to stop embracing the popular urban street terms like "savage", "hustler" the "N-word" ect. Instead of striving to be a savage there's a word with the same syllables ,same amount of letters from the French language "Savant" the definition is a person of profound or extensive learning, a learned scholar ,there's an African word "Negus"-The title of the supreme ruler of Ethiopia ....,subtle tweeks of the tounge destroys a stereotype and implements a distinguished persona ,   THINKING OUTSIDE the BLOCKS ....the name of this book recreates (minds of human beings) THINKING OUTSIDE THE BLOCKS navigated Ahmad through a life of humble beginnings ,criminality to evolving into the graduated student of North East High school in Philadelphia and also a college graduate of Temple University with a bachelor degree in secondary ed. English to owning multiple rental properties and owning an operating his own restaurant for over 15 years and now Inshallah bestselling author ,it's my overwhelming pleasure to introduce my brother

Mr. Ahmad Abdullah
THINK OUTSIDE the BLOCK enjoy the book join the movement!!! Look out for the Philly renaissance

INTRODUCTION

"THINKING OUTSIDE THE BLOCK

Thinking outside the block is a book following the mold of Dave Walkers Appeal published in 1829. David Walker was born (1796-1830) the son of an enslaved man and free African American woman, He was an entrepreneur, abolitionist, author and antislavery activist. His book "the Appeal "was a call for the people of color around the world to unite abolish slavery in America and injustice around the world to people of color. Similarly "Thinking outside the block" is a call for the Muslims in the united states starting in Philadelphia with African American community to unite to bring balance and justice to Philadelphia and beyond. Spreading throughout the whole world a spirit and message of unity and peace. We have an unique set of circumstances in Philadelphia regarding the Muslim community that can transform the lives of millions in a positive way. Also this is call for us to recognizes our potential for good and greatness in the world doing what is pleasing to our Lord in establishing justice on the earth. Fulfilling and living up to the Fitr (the natural order on which man was created) upon which He(Allah) created man to be a Khalifah(vicegerent- a person regarded as an earthly representative of God or a god). It is time to honor ourselves and the status given to us by the one who created us. I Appeal to my brothers and sisters in Islam first from African American decent but not limited to for we are all brothers and sisters in Islam regardless of nationality to move away from merely existing and moving at the pace set by entities other than Allah. Create a legacy of good in the world that will help to fill our graves with the same. Let us work towards leaving honorable mention on the tongues of the people. This world is hurting and in need of real leadership. The strength we possess in our mere presence and the influence we have on the world should be to move it in a direction of peace, unity and justice with dignity and honor. There is no need for a bullish take over I'm not talking going beast mode this establishment of justice peace and unity will take cooler heads emotion clouds reasoning love, anger frustration and the like all can affect your judgement. So with knowledge, self-assurance, purely good intention, faith, patience and perseverance. We can change the course of the world set better standards for ourselves and others since we are trend setters world-wide. Our ancestors in Africa created the blueprint which all the societies in the world were built on. Architecture, agriculture, medicine and science all that the world know of these things the foundation of them are of African origin. So, my people know who we are and our duty/responsibility to our Lord to establish justice and good in the land he created for us to rule and place high His name, Allah.

The Please touch museum in Philadelphia has a map of the city and on it pin-points the location of all the masjids in the city which says we are noticed and recognized so let's make our presence felt. Speaking with a brother he suggested a simple gesture that can go a long way and that is physically cleaning up the area around the masjids on a consistent bases. The trash in the area should be removed swept, bagged and set out for trash and even going as far as helping load trash onto sanitation truck when they come to collect. This gesture restores some pride in the community or the members of the community, changing their perspectives. Many of the masjids that were opened in Philadelphia are in areas or the ghettos, as recognized by many but we do not need to hold onto this mentality that the area is supposed to look uncared for because it is the hood or the ghetto, the block. Just as Islam has guided us on how to be purified from sin so should we be from some of these ignorant mentalities that many of us were raised upon. The responsibility to our neighbors is highly emphasized in our Religion (Sahih Muslim chapter42 Hadith2624 Surah Nisa ayat36) also keep in mind our prophet, may peace and blessings be upon him, was sent as a mercy to all of mankind so we should stick to following his example to the best of our ability and be a mercy to all of mankind also This gesture of cleaning up the area I reside or frequent brings to mind my brother from another mother Steve A.K.A. D.E.(Nadir may Allah be pleased with him),Who was also my partner in crime. He made a conscious effort to keep the block we hustled on swept and free of trash as a way to keep the neighbors a little more patient with the illegal activities we conducted on the block he would advise me of doing the same. So the idea of using this to have a positive impact on the communities surrounding the masjids and consequently the city is reasonable. I mean if it helped us with mischievous intentions with pure intentions we would achieve much greater results.

Along with David Walkers appeal another source of inspiration behind writing this book is a passage from one of my favorite books

" The Souls of black Folks" by W.E.B. Duu Bois published in 1903 where he states "**But when to earth is added an environment of men and ideas, then the attitude of the imprisoned group may take three main forms, a feeling of revolt or revenge; an attempt to adjust all thought and action to the will of the greater group ;or finally, a determined effort at self-realization and self-developement despite environing opnion.**"

This statement, from the book "The souls of Black folks", is one I first read ironically enough while in prison and it made me reflect and ask the question what group or category do we people of color fall under .I would argue we are of the 2nd group that is described as adjusting all thought and actions to the will of the greater group which the last part I will not concede to that the group we are adjusting thoughts and action to is greater than us, though I understand in that era the wording used by Du Bois . But none the less we should be of the 3rd group who makes a conscious and determined effort at "self-realization and self-development despite environing opinion",

Self -realization is the key we are not savages or beast. We take a clear untainted look at the role Africans have played. The contribution we have made to humanity over the throughout the world over the timespan of human existence we will see a much brighter picture. It was my recognition of this potential in myself that prompted me to write this appeal to myself fist to be a positive force in the world. Along with recognizing the potential I have also I see amongst brothers and sisters I know but it is not enough to know we must act in the best manner.

Section1

A mind is a terrible thing to waste

"A mind is a terrible thing to waste", this popular slogan was first created in 1972 to promote the United negro College Fund scholarship program for African American students by the advertising agency Young & Rubicam; it was successful in raising millions in scholarship funds, The slogan became popular because it is easy to apply to so many things and it has been used in different campaigns, referred to in films plus many other places. The slogan is easily applicable to many things cause of the amount of control the mind or the brain (these words I may use interchangeably) controls first starting with the body, the brain controls all bodily functions. At one point in time scientist believe the heart was the center of life for humans but later found it is the brain. True when the heart stops pumping it could mean the end of life for a human being but the signal, which tells the heart to stop beating comes from the brain.

Not only do the brain control all bodily functions, it also controls thoughts, ideas, perspectives which is equally important to human existence. These functions of the mind have an impact on the use and care of bodily functions so actually can be viewed as more important functions. Our minds are where we form our understanding of the world around us and our role in it. For this we must be really cautious of what we expose our minds to.

We can compare the brain to a computer and how the memory gets full we have to delete cookies and erase files to get it working at a normal speed, similarly the mind can get clogged when there's too much going on in it and clarity becomes hard to find but unlike a computer you cannot just push a button to get rid of information its extremely difficult if possible at all to unlearn something which makes what you learn to begin with so crucial.

Ivan Pavlov in his study of classical conditioning described a phenomenon he named spontaneous recovery that refers to previously extinguished conditioned response and or knowledge re-emerge after a delay or long period of time. Meaning we may learn new behaviors that suppress old behaviors or knowledge but without much effort previously learned knowledge or behaviors can reappear. The same goes for Perspectives that are formed at a young age and develop into a reality. That being said it is very important that we are mindful and watchful over what we expose or children to from our hands and mouths directly or indirectly. There is an intent, ideology and perspective behind every game, tv show, movie or anything else we make available to our youth, some are not so innocent, but may have malicious intent. So with that in mind lets monitor these things and not just consider them as something to entertain a child and keep their attention just to have a little free time from parenting to the contrary this a very Important aspect of parenting.

I lived for over ten years without television in my home for a few reasons one, I refused to pay for cable. I grew up in an era TV was free you paid for movies on Betamax or DVD's but not to watch basic channels secondly cable has so many channels you pay for and then turn around spend most of your time watching channels that were once free. Then on top of all that it is not possible to monitor all the shows that your children may come across. So, I eliminated the problem, yeah I would get DVD's that we could watch on my computer. I still was able to monitor wat was available to my children to watch after all I brought in the house or allowed it.

Perception=Reality

The media we allow our children to be influenced by can become their perception on life. Simply meaning it can be harmful to their lives all together understanding that our perception shapes and forms our realities. Far too often we laugh at some negative behaviors and characteristics from our youth that may later in life bring us to tears. We cannot blame all of this on entertainment and other outside entities we need to take full responsibility for the behavior and characteristics our children develop from the things we encourage and some we do not discourage. We like to tell our sons how bad they are with laughter encouraging this behavior instead of discouraging it. The older they get and become more defiant. The behavior becomes less and less amusing and humorous. It becomes dangerous harmful and alarming causing reason for concern every time they walk outside the home. That characteristic found once humorous in your home may not be received the same way by folks outside your home likewise the patience and tolerance of the disruptive behavior won't be the same. We like to encourage physical toughness but forget about mental and spiritual strength which supersedes physical strength in every arena should be the strength promoted along with high moral value and character given the attention that is well deserving to nurture strong men who are well seasoned. Our daughters need to be not only sheltered and protected from physical harm, but a great deal of protection is needed to protect their character and honor. There is a famous quote **"If you teach a boy you educate an individual; but if you teach a girl you educate a whole community** ".Our daughters will one day grow to be the mothers in our community that will give birth to and help raise other girls and boys. Our Women are the first educators of our youth and for that reason our daughters must be prepared to protect and elevate our community. This is in no way a lightening of the load a man must carry in raising a child to build a strong community because his impact is unmeasurable. Mary Mcleod Bethune stated "**The true value of a race must be measured by the character of its womenhood**".

Spoiling our children

Another serious matter that needs to be reconsidered regarding raising our youth is the notion they need to be adorned with all the latest fashion sparing no cost. Many times the case is we're looking to live vicariously through our children with material things that our parents may have not been able to afford to or just were unwilling to get us at a young cause their values were different. Some of our parents come from generation where struggle and poverty took on a different meaning from what it is today. Many of the citizen in the U.S. are spoiled rich kids when compared to some other nations. The idea of spending a lot of money on sneakers and other clothing is unfathomable to some poor communities in other nations, but travel threw just about any neighbor in America that's considered low income or poor and you'll find residents there with Jordan sneakers, who haven't made a new pair of sneakers in 30 years but go up on the price when he reintroduce a sneaker from 1990's in a different color. You will also find children with I phones, tablets and many other things that you would not expect for individuals saying they're from the slums and don't have much.

The nation economy and job market was not the same and still differs especially for minorities. The job market for minorities was so marginalized at one point that high priced fashion was not a priority for many generations above putting food on the table and not from restaurants either home cooked meals were standards eating out was occasional, and not the occasion you were hungry and had a taste for a particular meal so they ordered it or ran out to get it. Whatever was being made is what we ate, and it taste better than hunger. Our thoughts and opinion on what were to be served was not always considered, there was no poll taken on what was for diner. it was what dad brought home and mom cooked period or you can be hungry which was not reasonable so we ate what was there and was thankful for what was made available to us .We wouldn't dare frown our faces up and complain about not being pleased with what were provided to eat and expect no consequences as I've seen far too often today .As if they child provided and prepared the meal. Ultimately this is ungratefulness to our Lord for the provisions we have been given.

The cost of living was not equal to what it is today but has risen equally to or greater than the increase in income and wages nation-wide. So even as there has been creation of more well -paying jobs and the rise of minimum wages the cost of food and housing has increased as well which keeps many Americans at the same level they've been for decades and then to add to that clothing transportation and entertainment the cost of living has multiplied . We are creating appetites for our children that will increase and be terribly difficult for them to satisfy when they get older and having to care for themselves and a family possibly. How do we teach them to save and create a budget for businesses that can stabilize and advance our communities in these growing times. When they are shown too often that material/fashionable gains are of such great value. Staying trendy or in the now makes such a great difference on your existence is the message. It is terrible how material things are used to negotiate good behavior and we reward our children for doing wrong with $100 sneakers and then turn around get upset when the sneakers are messed up quickly. We cannot and should not attempt to buy/bribe good behavior from our children, The cost of living increases every year and to keep up with fashion trends on top of it is doable but how reasonable is it in all honesty. In a moment of quietness, clarity and honesty Reflect on the tendencies/desires we have to be fashionable "in the now" with everything and question yourself on how with discipline and a purpose beyond yourself and today what you could you achieve of bigger goals than self. For this I say to anyone we are not a poor race of people it is our planning and priorities that are poor and misplaced. Too often we feel like these things add value to who we are as a person when truthfully speaking it is not the case. When we understand our value as people individually and collectively we'll realize all that has ever given us our value is internal not external the morals and values that has given honor to those who came before us will preserve and restore us to the place we belong.

Section 2

Development/Progress

When we develop a mindset of planning for our children's children to have and be disciplined on achieving this goal collectively it will really be the dawn of a new day with better days being ahead!!! And Allah knows best. There must be a change in approach towards life and our outlook on what we hold or define as successful the way we have been going about this, in my generation at least, I'll say has not progressed us in ways we are capable of. So how much longer must we settle and our communities suffer from not building a solid foundation for our youth to build on . Is the fear of change that great? As if this is so satisfying to everyone in this era we are in or is it because we can point out a handful of people who have achieved some financial success we feel like a new day has already come upon us? Collectively with discipline, loyalty, dignity and commitment to a common goal we could acquire generational wealth.

Today we have an overload of information we can find a better way. Then the question comes about of our commitment to progress which should be the goal. This we'll find the key to looking back in our history over the lifespan of mankind. We have been spinning our wheels in the mud far too long let us get to moving our community forward the world needs us to help to bring balance and justice to it. We are far too influential people to not recognize and make it that our influence on the world be honorable and not just entertaining especially in ways that insult our honor and dignity. The time is now for us to get unstuck from this mud that we have been spinning our wheels in for too long clean up and shine bright like we were created to do.

The internet with all the potential good and necessity now day pose is equally if not more potentially harmful to our youth it is far too easily assessable to our children they walk around with in their pockets and hands all day via cell phones. Social media and reality tv show are detrimental to our youth forming and shaping the perspectives/realities of many today. Parents have to really remain conscious of these harms and be diligent in monitoring how much exposure their child have to these things and finding alternatives to them in order to minimize the influence it has on our youth Creating book clubs at home with their children and their friends along with other parents opening dialogue to combat many of the ideologies our children are being exposed to. Outdoor activities to help engage them with life on an earth surface level. It is not enough to just take a phone away as if that will stop them from being affected by these things.

Collective efforts in a communal way to raise our youth is more of a dire need more than ever. We have moved so far away from a village mentality and our youth is suffering. We have been in a crisis in our community for decades. Some would even say since we were first brought to this country. Crisis in Chinese means danger and also means opportunity. I want us to focus on the opportunity more than the danger of the of the crisis we've been in we have an opportunity to transform the culture and mindsets of the community we are in . Those of us ,talking about myself first, who negatively affected the mindset and culture in communities we grew up in looking to be leaders, trendsetters and the like . Should feel responsible to clean up some of the mess we made. We can create a new type of renaissance in African American or just American history (**renaissance-a revival or renewed interest in something; synonyms -resurgent ,re-emergence, resurrection, rebirth)** so).So let us look at or create our vision for a community we're responsible for building for our children and generations to come. This is the example of our messenger and his companions and those who followed them in good. The prophet Muhammad, May peace and blessings be upon him, was sent as a mercy to all of mankind so should we be also. So what will we contribute to our communities and the world seeing how communities has become global with the internet the ease of travel and communication a person can travel back and forth between countries even continents in a day when before it would have taken months or years .We can make phone calls or send messages even faster, instantly when before it took a very long time.

Those in my age bracket of mid to late forty's or over can remember growing up in communities where you could be chastised by elders in the community on your way to be further reprimanded by your parents .This was the love and concern they showed from one block to the next. In my neighborhood growing up as a kid I remember feeling like the whole neighborhood was my extended family. For blocks and blocks I could go sit at the table and eat at just about any house on any block we considered part of the neighborhood even homes that's wasn't of my friend they may have just been friends of my parents or other relatives. It was not strange to come home and see a friend of mines or a neighbor sitting on the couch or at the table eating and socializing with my family as if they lived there. Let me reflect even more direct and in detail still those in my age bracket can really relate and remember our neighborhoods before crack cocaine tore us apart and made us susceptible to just about anything. We saw our neighborhoods go from being filled of people energized regardless of living below poverty levels. Children filling up the streets playing, summer times were always enjoyable, now I cannot paint a totally pretty picture as if no crime and commotion was around before crack came but there was a life and energy around that cannot be described to someone who has not experienced its joy. In the early to mid-eighties much of that life was inhaled from our communities threw a glass pipe and grey clouds exhaled over them even those bright sunny summer days.

Again, its not to say that crime didn't exist there was still some discretion about it and an attempt to keep some things hidden from the whole neighborhood. The underground world was really underground. Crack came and destroyed much of that. Shame and discretion went out the door along with pride and dignity, self-respect and self- realization , Not only was the drugs sold out in the open there was no hiding an individual's involvement in that life. For the dealers it brought about a status and cash flow that was not intended to be hidden not even always from the police. That is because thousands of dollars passed through the hands of young people on daily basis which altered the perspectives/realities of life and what It was all about. The zeal of the youth without the proper patience and guidance of their elders mixed with a lot of money and power is a harmful potion. This deadly combination has helped lead us to what we are seeing now not just In philly, **gentrification**-the process of renovating a house or district so that it conforms to middle class taste) I remember being informed of the gentrification coming to my neighborhood back in 1996 a barmaid who worked at the bar on the corner of the block I hustled on became really good friends. She would call me the son she wished she had I made sure she was safe leaving at night would even drop her off at times when she didn't drive there or didn't have a ride, there were nights she closed early cause I told her I would not be in the neighborhood that evening, she worked at the Philadelphia planning commission in the daytime and asked me to come by to meet a guy at her job. I did and he began to tell me how my neighborhood would not be my neighborhood in the next five years or so. You see much of the planning for new construction and change to such a degree as it has come about it planned out years before going into work. Even after hearing this I could not fathom it would change to such a degree in which it has. The gentleman offered to help me obtain some real estate the area which at the time had not yet begun to be nearly as expensive as it is today. I called myself making some changes to get ready for what was coming signed up to go to community college majoring in business, began looking up properties as he advised. There was one major change I did not make and that was leaving the streets alone and expanding the circle around me or getting the help of friends and elders to start this new life venture. Not six months after meeting with this gentleman I was arrested in early part of 1997 which changed my life considerably after being released I moved from the neighborhood lost touch with friends and money. By the time I was able to start back inquiring about the real estate market in the neighborhood had begun to take off beyond my financial and mental means at the time. There was one property I had my sights set on I knew the family that previously lived there. The house had been abandoned for many years a realtor had a for sale sign on it I called inquiring about it they were asking eighty thousand for it as is. The guy I knew at planning commission passed away I went down there one day looking for him seeking some direction of where to invest even if not in my own neighborhood but another that was up and coming area.

Correction, I first heard about gentrification like many of you might have from the movie Boyz In The Hood When Lawrence Fishbourne was educating his son played by Cuba Gooding jr.. and others about gentrification standing in front of BUILD BORD ASKING PEOPLE TO SALE THEIR HOMES.

Another one mistake of mine was holding onto and not realizing how vital the information I was given was, a mistake a lot of us make. There were leaders in my community I'm sure some knew about the   changes to come because of their political affiliation, and other ties. They also held onto information that could have benefitted the community. I was young at the time, not to make an excuse for myself, around 23. I blame my affiliation with the streets and not " Thinking outside the block" for missing out on an opportunity to help myself and those close to me to acquire wealth preserve our place in our neighborhood which we love . I write this today not with a defeated mindset as if the only opportunity I had has been lost, no I am writing today realizing the opportunity is at hand which we must collectively cease and make the best of. This time is even better for me and those closes to me cause of Islam and the Sunnah. With the proper intention and following the example of those who came before us the messenger , his companions, and those from the early generation who followed them in good sticking to the clear and correct guidance to build a community based on values found in Islam.

Section 3

Neglect

Carter G Woodson stated "if you can make a man feel that he is inferior, you don't have to compel him to accept an inferior status he will seek it himself"

This process of gentrification has been made so easy by our own hands we handed our neighbor hoods over to Outsiders who saw blocks with buildings that could make a lot money in a much different way than we were accustomed to making money from them. Once the new construction started and the value OF THE HOMES BEING BUILT were set so high along with the existing homeowners property taxes going up many people felt hopeless if they wanted to stay not being able to afford to do so. Now a days many of us may feel like an outsider in the communities we grew up in. The changes gentrification brought about in my neighborhood and others around the city at first intriguing to see. As it revealed itself further I was no longer intrigued or impressed neither will I say depressed but it leaves an ill taste I feel we gave the outsiders our neighborhoods gift wrapped cause we couldn't "think outside the block" we called my hood Moroccos ,which was the gang the governed it since the sixties, the city named it Francisville, much of the identity that made my neighborhood, my neighborhood has faded away. Not only are the houses being transformed a lot of the residence that made it my hood are gone some moved many passed young and old. What once was my community is now just a neighborhood there is a big difference between the two .**This is why I dedicate this book to them.** My parents are still in the area which keeps my frequenting the area. I lost being impressed also because I feel we should've been   pro-active in changing the culture in our communities. Not to dwell on what has transpired I am inspired by the opportunity at hand and want to encourage us to regroup and pull together all that we have learned from the past thirty years or so and began to plan and build communities around the masjids in Philadelphia. Make the communities desirable to live in creating an environment that is safe and warm, loving and nurturing the right minds to maintain and further advance our communities productivity

There is though a specific area of the city I am particularly fond of and plan to hold another event with other investors, entrepreneurs and elicit as many likeminded people to put a plan together to build a strong community for colored people led by the Muslims. I held a networking event there in 2015 there's not much around there, but that's the point and what makes it so intriguing I believe it could serve as an example for other communities to build. Now I know I first said build around existing masjids but we may need to really "Think outside the block" build one from the ground up doing the same for a school in an area close to masjid. Solicit doctors to open OBGYN and health clinics with at least one to be ran by women the whole staff may not be Muslim but it gives Muslim women the comfort of going to a doctor's office uncover while there and not have to worry any male staff including sanitation. This will take some years in planning so some of our wives and daughters may need to obtain medical degrees, become doctors, certified nurses and other professions in the health field dentist etc. have a whole building dedicated to our women and their health the first floor and basement be for security to protect our women children who are the future of our community. Just as I mentioned about gentrification it takes years of planning before coming to existence. This is all attainable we are very resourceful people and collectively serving a communal goal with good intentions leaving our ego's aside, Which an acronym for is (**E**liminating **G**od **O**ut). It is time to make our presence felt. Done correctly our communities will be marveled and respected world wide. Why can't we create a community in Philadelphia known for its rich Islamic culture and heritage? In just about every major city in America there is a Chinatown. In Manhattan we have Little Italy and other places around the country are none for a particular culture. the Amish has acquired land built a communities and have laws that govern their communities. In Pennsylvania there is a section that recognize the school curriculum they have which differs from the rest of the state mandated curriculum.

I remember back in 2006 at Germantown masjid which is now masjid as Sunnah annabawiyyah). The then imam Daud Adib gave a very serious lecture tittled "From Germantown to Muslimtown" urging the community to make a conscious effort to build a community around the masjid with schools and other businesses in the area. Now this lecture was given over a decade ago and we may still be a decade or so away from this seriously taking place, though there are signs of it happening in the area the type of communities that we need to establish should go beyond just the Germantown section of Philadelphia cause there are masjids in various neighborhoods around the city and the community or whole city should benefit from the presence of Islam The one simple gesture mentioned in the introduction will make our presence felt and also propagate Islam, cleaning up the streets around the masjids on a consistent basis. There could be a designated day of the month coordinated between all the masjids and city officials that on, for example, the third Saturday of every month this city wide clean up done by the Muslims in the city in the neighborhood they reside in would speak volumes as we are showing kindness to our neighbors as we are advised to do by the messenger Muhammad(may peace and blessings be upon him), who also explained moving something harmful out the way is an act of charity He(may the peace and blessings of Allah be upon him)advised his ummah(community) often about tending to the needs of their nieghbors. Let us be charitable and dutiful to our neighbors by not just cleaning up the neighborhood physically but help clean up the mentality of the community and inner city, which many of the masjids in Philadelphia are located. The ideology that because it is the inner city a.k.a ghetto its suppose to look run down and unkept, not cared for by the residence of the area is not one we should hold.

Ghetto is not a location more than it is a mentality **Ghetto-"a part of a city, especially a slum area, occupied by a minority group or groups". Slum"-a squalid or overcrowded urban street or district inhabited by very poor people. SQualid- (of a place) extremely dirty**

and unpleasant as a result of poverty or neglect. ". Now under these definitions of ghetto are we willing to accept and take pride in it describing where we live worship and raise our children. It is not so that we wait or look for the city to come in and clean up and maintain where we live and worship. they will only to solicit investors who will change dynamics of the area as we already see happening. Right or wrong has no place in this conversation cause it will not change how things go it is, what it is. We must be responsible for our communities and advance them beyond these definitions and expectations.

Carter G. Woodson stated "if you can control a man's thinking you never have to worry about his actions"

The mindset of many of the residence in urban areas need to be resurrected from having dead and unproductive citizens to lively vibrant communities producing creative minds to develop better communities and world. The circumstances surrounding poverty for African Americans in this country over the years has impacted the way of thinking, operating in society and the relationships with each other.

We need to develop and change our mindset from being led or driven by entertainment to being motivated by achieving goals like creating our own economy. We hear all the time about how long the black dollar stays in our community as apposed to other communities and how they spend with each other.

My daughters once were planning a dinner with friends and asked me about a few different restaurant in the city. They named a few I suggested they go to South street a diverse commercial street with a variety of stores and restaurants there are a few owned by an African Americans there was one in particular I recommended I told them when they do to take a look around and take an account of the number of people they see from outside our race. The numbers are small but reverse the same scenario and watch how much the numbers grow. Now the amount of traffic South Street has on any given night of individuals from many different racial backgrounds would have one to suspect the patrons of the businesses would reflect the diversity of culture that travels the street. Why is that we are so supportive of others but will not receive or demand the same support. In too many cases we'll support others over our own which just blows my mind.

    I operated a café for 15 years in an urban community that is highly populated by people of color   I saw day after day people from the neighborhood walk past some would even stop to talk but would not come in to support they would go down the street to a Korean owned doughnut shop that sold breakfast and lunch supporting them unconditionally. My menu was more elaborate than theirs I sold breakfast platters they just sold sandwiches. my lunch and dinner platters were more mature than burgers and fries that the other place sold I do not believe my prices were too high I knew the area I was in and priced the menu accordingly plus I can cook and the food was good. We need to develop the mentality of seeking out our own to support in business. It is a practice of many other cultures to recycle their money within their community. Equally we should support one another in personal matters,along with bussinessmatters. This support in business could help many households of individuals who own and operate these businesses along with the employees. The ripple effect could resonate out far in our communities. Something that can not be said for business owners in our neighborhoods who are not African American. Case in point the area where my café was there was a dollar store around the corner that was supported heavily by the community and one year was asked to donate a cases of water to the little league football team the store owner was reluctant to along with the doughnut shop until one of the elders stood outside their store with a picket sign discouraging patrons from supporting them .due to lack of support for the team, a practice which I made a routine of doing one reason being the business that I received and sure other businesses received as a result of the games played in the park and the traffic it produced made it easy to help out with something simple as cases of water, but many of the businesses in our community don't share the connection to the community I did even though it was not a neighborhood I grew up in I connected with it cause there were many similarities to my community I did grow up in The most obvious and prevailing was ethnicity. I could see myself and friends threw these young African American boys playing football like we did at that age only thing differed is there teams was organized with a city wide league ours was unofficial with a limited involvement from other neighborhoods. I think it's a good thing the football and baseball organizations in the community given children some structure and positive things to do, but we must plan and create programs outside of entertainment for our youth for our communities to progress.

The mindset of playing for a team instead of owning limits our community control over an industry that profits so much off our labor. This goes for music tv and movies also. Sports and music are two of the industries that affect the culture in urban communities and all around the world.

Ahmad Abdullah

Sports

Football and basketball are the two leading sports that influence a lot of the culture in America , especially in African American communities . We take a look at the recent attempt at social reform from the stands or kneeling of the former quarterback of San Francisco 49's Colin Kapernick and raise a few question had all the African American players took a knee our true power over the Negro, Football, Leauge would have been revealed the NFL without people of color would not have half the financial value it has today. The proof is before the league was integrated back in 1946. Before then there were only 13 African Americans players in whole league the revenue and influence on American culture from this entity was nothing near what it is today largely in part due to men of color. today the league is 75%African American. The projected revenue for N.F.L. over next five years is to reach upwards to twenty five billion dollars annually. Largely due to the African American players and yet there is not one African American owner. So had the African American along with Latino players in the NFL saw the crises as an opportunity for financial freedom and not a danger to their profession pulled their resources created their own league the fans and investors would've followed them .It would've been difficult. Took years of legal battles but with the world looking a quicker resolution would've been best for those who control the league now.

Then the next and greater task would have been controlling the culture of the league that would've been created and the influence it would have on the rest of the world.to take ownership of the talent and skills these players poses by the players go beyond making sure it produce wins on game day. The responsibility of the players to the fans who support them especially the youth that look up to them and immolate much of what they see from on and off the field. This responsibility should not be neglected even now. Just the thought of a league that is made up of predominately African American players and not one single owner of a team sounds crazy and is by design.The current owners in the league must vote an agree to let new owner in even if the individual has the money to buy a team An industry we have taken to heights it would not have reached without us has not one owner of a team who is African American should not be so surprising we barely can get a head coach in this industry. The entity has been set up like the entity we call the United States of America which has laws that were designed to limit the growth of our community but with a closer look there are laws that will support our plight.   Self sufficient is what we must become in all areas of our existence.

Music

Music is another highly influential area of entertainment that has been pioneered and taken to heights that may have been unfathomable in the beginning even as I imagine the dream was to make it big by many who started the industry, speaking about rap music in particular. I can recall rap music at its birth we both were youths growing at the same time rap music or hip hop birth coming in the early 70's and during this time the many of the songs had a positive message or told stories. "The Message" the title to a popular song by Grandmaster flash that came out in the 70's speaking about social injustice following the tradition of music of colored people in America dating back to times of slavery. The songs sang were of hope looking forward to better days than the ones they were living threw. Slaves didn't sing praises or glorify the horrors of physical abuse ,rape and murder they were living through as if it was cool, but this is what they knew and was living, the argument many rappers put forth when explaining why their lyrics depict so much negativity. They say this is what they know or been exposed to growing up. Today the music has been overridden by glorifying the crime and horrors of today with little of hopes for a better tomorrow aside from money, received threw criminal sources being the major theme of the music, as if that alone will be our salvation. The killing of our own people along with drugs and violence made to be THATLIFE!!! also with degrading our women as if it is really honorable. We can and must do better at the representation we portray to the world taking into consideration the influence we have on the world it would be in our best interest to make it positive and desirable for other nation to want to affiliate themselves with us for more than sports and entertainment purpose.

Actually that is not just the responsibility of the entertainment industry, though they do have a responsibility to correctly represent our culture, but these industries has been manipulated by, conniving individuals who chose to stay behind the scenes do to their evil Intentions for profit, portraying African Americans in a particular manner which that does not highlight our true nature, but serves their agenda.

Indoctrination

Indoctrination -the process of teaching a person or group of to accept a set of beliefs uncritically.

"The conscious and intelligent manipulation of the organized habits and opinions of the masses is an important element in democratic society . Those who manipulate this unseen mechanism of society constitute an invisible government which is the true ruling power of our country. We are governed, our minds are molded, our tastes formed our ideas suggested, largely by men we have never heard of."

Edward Bernays

Edward Bernays, the nephew of Sigmund freud, also none as the father of propaganda, has helped orchestrate the manipulation of the minds of the masses at the request of the governments during the time of wars to come up with campaigns to justify going to war to civilians. Big business has employed his services to market products to a particular sector of society for example when the cigarette industry sought his aid in marketing to women who were not buying cigarettes when they were first being sold .He advised cigarette makers to pay debutantes, which would be equivalent to todays divas, to go into a public place dressed nice sit smoke cigarettes and look to have a good time. Newspapers and other media outlets were tipped off to document the day which made smoking look cool amongst women and started the growth in sales to women. This is the same type of marketing sceems being used today   Edward Bernays became a very wealthy man from his propaganda tactics . Propaganda is still a very profitable tactic used by government and businesses big or small alike. We as citizens and consumers need to be conscious of the tactics to not be fooled. One of the things businesses profited most from was how Bernays marketing techniques could get individuals to buy things they didn't need which plagues our society today basically greed!! .This is a country of spoiled rich children our so called poverty stricken citizens dress fashionably dine out more than just occasionally and have things citizens in other countries who are in poverty would considered luxuries we buy things we don't need far too often then at times find we didn't want them as much as we thought. Fashion is a place you find this happening a lot this industry is so trendy and displays our undying desire for things we don't need paying hundreds of dollars on sneakers or shoes that will not last a season do to wear and tear or change in fashion trends. We cannot really say how much of what we think or how we view things are solely do to our own thoughts opinions and ideas. They are an accumulation of the knowledge and experiences we gathered up to this point in our lives which have been influenced in many ways some we can identify and admit to others we may deny or can't detect. None the less it is there and our brains cannot be erased or information deleted and start the process all over again like computers but as humans we have the capacity to progress, grow and evolve. There is a growth that takes place in human perspective every five to seven years behavioral scientist label as stages of development. These stages are impacted in many ways

Marketing and advertisement is such an important industry to the retail market in which they pay advertisers very well to give strategies on how to market products on a short term and long term basis to specific target groups as well as the mases. These strategies are very effective in manipulating sales to the target audience our thoughts ideas and opinions are cleverly manipulated along with what is made available to us. This is also the case with other industries like music.

The radio will tell you they're giving the people what they want or request, though a real variety is not made available to the listeners with an opportunity to decide what genre of music they would like to hear.

As a teen growing up with hip hop, I say with cause its birth came around the same time as mines, there were different genres not all was plagued with the same themes Criminal immoral lyrics that falsely represented a lifestyle many who rap about do not and should not live. In thi era that lives off the term "keeping it real or 100". That rhetorical question, "is life imitating art or art imitating life?" is not a blurred lined as much as the question may make it seem. There is a purpose behind having these ideas, opinions, values etc. promoted by a very influential sector of society to affect the lives being lived by listeners or followers. Some of what is shared can be truth hyperbolized either way it impacts the thoughts of the listeners and onlookers who form opinions on the listeners based on lyrics that may or may not truly represent them honestly. The imagery portrayed desensitize the hearts and minds of listeners on the lyrics and lifestyle promoted by the rap culture that has been infiltrated to bring about this negative outlook on a culture that in the late 80's early 90's started to become a voice of revolution and change for the youths. This did not suit the agenda of those who own radio stations and other entities that profit off criminal mentality prevailing among certain groups of society. Entities like private prison that profit greatly from the promotion of the criminal mode of thinking and conduct. To continue reflecting on the statement from Edward Bernayse this manipulation is with malice intent serving the agenda of men whose faces we may never see nor individuals in the industry.

Ahmad Abdullah

Prison is not a right of passage

<u>**Right sof passage** -is a ceremony or ritual of passage that occurs when an individual leaves one group to enter another.it involves a significant change of status in society.' In every culture there are events that mark the change of an individual from one stage to the next. From childhood to an adulthood like being able to drive , vote and the like .</u>

For far too long going to jail has become or viewed as a right of passage in our communities. I remember when my lil brother was arrested and when he finally came home my mom asked why all the traffic was coming to her door and the rise of celebration amongst his friends around the corner. I explained to her that he is now accepted on the block made official he part of the gang, This ideology of prison being a right of passage is put on display in Goodfellas, when Henry Hill went to jail and did not tell. This scene from the movie, is highly dramatized cause I never seen such a celebration of any youth in my neighborhood being released from jail maybe after doing some time but not just for being locked up and bailed out the for the first time, it depicts a disoriented mentality advertised to people of color and Latinos.

The only thing the united states leads the world in is the number of citizens incarcerated. There are a handful of countries, Auatraiia , u.k., Canada the United States that allow prisons to be for profit, but we still lead on the percentage of citizens incarcerated .

Pennsylvania alone has 27 state penitentiaries that is more than the number of state collages in Pennsylvania with more penitentiaries being built. For profit prisons have a long history in the united states dating back to 1852 When San Quentin was built but today is state owned. Ironically private prisons came into existence not long after slavery was said to have been abolished and the thirteenth amendment created stating "Neither slaver nor involuntary servitude, except as a punishment for crime whereof the party shall have been duly convicted, shall exist within the United States , or any place subject to their jurisdiction. This was a nation realizing they were about to lose out on the most significant economic commodity that made America a strong economic country, Free labor!!!.It seems like the country was looking to hold onto free labor anyway possible and for long as possible. Profiting off others kindness or misfortune ignorance is woven into the fabric of America from its very conception. Knowing this and continuously fallen prey to it is not to but the blame on society responsibility falls on us.

The negative impact of leaving our children when going to jail is unmeasurable. Our sons not having a positive example to follow of how to earn a righteous living being a loyal and honorable husband,father. We lose out being an example to our daughters of what a good husband and father to their children look like. We keeping a dysfunctional cycle of our sons following our example becoming inmates our daughters getting caught in a the web of boys who weren't taught what manhood really means is a trend that must stop. Men get upset when their children are not brought up to prison to visit them not mindful of how upset the children are for not seeing them on a regular basis and the pain or empty feeling of walking out of the jail after a visit. There's no honor in going to jail no matter how theatrical the movies depict it or cool the beat to the rap song mentioning being locked up. Not even the homie that come home with stories laughing and joking like it was such a great adventure.

I just recently attended a court hearing in support of a very good childhood friend I came up from the sandbox with. He was at the sentencing stage where and his record was read by the judge his two daughters, mother and sister were asked to speak to help seek leniency from the judge when the weight of this sad cycle hit me. The judge read his record starting with a juvenile offense in 1990 one of his daughters who is now 24 stated her father went to jail when she was one and has been in and out of there for19 years of her life. He was asked by the judge to explain why she should show leniency because it seems as if he has not learned anything from incarceration. The pain I felt on their behalf I'm sure could not match any of theirs. It is not a passage if you repeat the process. It contradicts the meaning of the word passage- **the act or process of moving through, under, over, or past something on the way from one place to another**

Going to prison is not a place to go to regroup start deening, or reconnecting with Islam our work as Muslims men as well as women is at home with our families. Prison is not to be looked at as mount Hira, where the prophet (may peace and blessings of Allah be on him) would go to seclude himself from the disbelief in Mecca before Islam and where he first received revelation. Unlike this being in those mountains will not bring a divine decree as it did prophet Muhammad, peace and blessings be upon him, or like that of Musa(Moses), upon him be peace, where he was led to and spoken to directly by Allah and given the commandments. There will be no revelation sent down to any penitentiary in America or anywhere else regardless of the mountain.

The Pocono mountains have hotels resorts and many things to do all year long you can take your children and enjoy I've taken mines on more than one occasion better to go when its warm can enjoy outdoors. I went during a july4th weekend had a ball swimming horseback riding and other outside activities. I went during my children's Christmas break from school got cabin fever was too cold to be outside for long could not even enjoy the ski slopes.

Need an escape to the mountains take a trip with the family so you all can enjoy the visit not have family members travel hours into the mountains to spend an hour sitting a room with a bunch of other families going through the same anguish. The time could be used to clear your head focus on what really matters, those who accompanied you on the trip and your Lord. Make time to supplicate to Him (Rabbil ka'bah)make it a routine trip to strengthen the bind with your family and your Lord like going to prison for some is a routine. It is imperative we do better for the sake of our souls and those we're responsible for. Allah says in the Qur'an to save yourselves and families from the fire(surah 66:verse6) how can we do so committing crimes and abandoning our families going to prison.

The argument of not having no other choice is no longer a defense Islam has destroyed it so let us be believing men some cases believing women fear our Lord and the meeting with Him keeping ourselves obedient to His laws at the same time staying within the law of the land. My brothers and sisters please let leave off the mentality we have from jahaliyah (days of ignorance before Islam) do as we were commanded and enter into Islam whole heartedly. It pains me and I'm embarrassed even with nobody else in the room to see on the news a shooting or other criminal activity reported they show the individuals face he has a beard as big or bigger than mines. Allah a said we are the best of mandkind our conditions should reflect that title given to us. That can only be done by observing the condition Allah has placed to carry the title, and when I say our condition should reflect I don't mean monetarily. The code of conduct in which we carry ourselves interacting with each other and those outside of our ranks.

Section 4

World Impact

It is the responsibility of all of us to restore an reset the train back on track in this land and beyond e, o especially with the land we came from. There has always been a conscious effort to keep this reconstructing of a connection between African Americans and Africa from happening. The strength this unity could build would be monumental. All the worlds natural resources are in Africa it is full of wealth. We African American have a courage and strength to overcome and withstand any obstacle that comes our way we are more powerful than we realize. Our influence on the world is undeniable.

I remember once being in Dubai mall at the Adidas store the young lady working there cam e over to help me and asked where I was from after saying America she got hype kept repeating "I knew it!!!" excited to meet a brother from America. She told me there was a word we used she wanted to understand it better but she couldn't remember what it was til I was almost out the door the word was "swagga" I explained it describes ones presences body, language as well as dress code .I said to her that she was drawn to me when I came in the store and asked to help me cause my swagga is nice and stood in a stands of pride she almost could not contain her joy and excitement from a brief my response and a brief encounter with an African American the like of which she probably only seen on her tv ,ınternet or heard on radio. Another occasion while in Dubai I was stopped on the train platform there by an officer who asked for my I.D. After showing my state I.D. he said American that's it I laughed and said you don't see many of my kind do you he smirked and handed my license back and walked away. My presences moved him before I walked past him he was lounging against the wall looking bored at the but as I walked past he raised up off the wall stood alert gathered himself before approaching me. I didn't take offense to it like why me out of everyone around he stops I'm intrigued by the reception I receive when I get to travel outside the country I encourage us all to do as much traveling as possible and not just take the approach as a tourist just passing through wanting to see the tourist attraction.

Go where the locals live go see how they live. Become open to learn the culture from within. The views , values and perception of the locals. I make it my business to sit amongst the locals and get their view of the land I'm in and the land where I'm from. You can never know what you may learn and can teach from the correspondence. so try it next time you travel outside theses states get a since of what the perception and influence we have on the world see what positivity you can add to it and the potential benefits that can come from it. This is how we take control of the perception and influence we have around the world.

In a greater matter Allah has charged us with the responsibility of helping to establish His religion in this land from the Strength and influence we have on this land and consequently the world, by His permission. We have made it by the permission of Allah comfortable for Muslims from other countries to come here and no longer fear having the outward appearance of Islam like beards, Islamic clothing for men and women. We should look at this as a responsibility and fully step up to the plate and establish a strong well balanced community. In a city like Philadelphia where we are recognized in other places in the states and around the world in Islamic communities for being a city where Islamic knowledge is strong.

I was in Chicago once and the brother I was went out there to see took me to a masjid for salat. While waiting for prayer he introduced me to a couple of his friends and mentioned I was from Philadelphia at which time a brother sitting not far away moved close to me introduced himself and began telling me how he was interested in going to the university in Madinah and was told Philly was a good place to go in order to get in there . I was impressed by the outlook of my city this brother wanted to get university of Madinah via Philly which speaks volume to how Philadelphia is perceived to the Muslim world.

Another instance that stands out is when I was favored by Allah and was given the means to make Hajj in 2009 as we are commanded to once in our lifetime, something I also encourage all of my brothers and sisters to do for the benefits of performing this act of worship and the reward we're promised by Allah in the hereafter and the benefit it has on your perspective in this life. It has forever changed my outlook on life while I was at the Ka'abah there was a brother making tawaf (circumambulating around the ka'bah)as I was and just looking at me said you from Philly aren't you smiled and kept walking it was so shocking to me I just let him keep walking I have no idea where he was from but he was confident and accurate about my origins So we could really make a difference in the world from Philadelphia and the Muslim communities here having a common goal of establishing a strong Islamic community in the city to be recognized all over the world.

It is not uncommon in Philadelphia to walk into any workplace and see a Muslim man or women with the outward appearance of Islam, thobe big beards woman with niqabs and abiyyahs gloves the full package. It is important in monitoring the things that will influence the perception which shapes the reality of our youth and their role and responsibility as Muslim.

Their responsibilities along with potential needs to be clearly outlined so they don't fall into being boys from the hood who wear thobes, pants cut above the ankles and big beards, or women who just wear over garments and khimars but no real understanding of who they are and their role and responsibility in life as vicegerents .Representing Allah's religion 'His justice, His mercy, His kindness on earth. We have an opportunity and responsibility to pioneer the building of a community here in the U.S. like no other place in the country. One that might be viewed as the Mecca of the West hosting Muslims from the U.S. or neighboring Western countries looking to learn more about islam and ways to build communities in their community.

Properly educating our youth

It is imperative that our youth are equipped with a well -balanced education to prepare them as well as possible for all the evils that will await them as they grow and venture out on their own establishing homes for their families. First and foremost establishing a firm foundation and understanding of who their Lord is with correct knowledge of His religion and the example of His last prophet ,may peace and blessings be upon him, with the correct understanding of his companions and those who follow them. On top of that our youth need more positive imagery on our lineage and history there are so many negative messages in society on what it means being African American or black is it will affect how they see themselves even as Muslims.

I remember teaching a class to 5th and 6th grade students where I covered early African Kingdoms of the sub-saharan. I had a student transfer late in the lesson to my class I was reviewing all that I covered and he honestly and sincerely asked me how could we be kings when we were slaves. It hurt me to hear this question and how genuinely it was confusing to him I sat next to him and put my hand on his shoulder and explained our lineage and history does not begin with slavery. I explained that there are prophet's messengers and many men of honor and nobility that are of African descent. The even more heartbreaking part to this story is it was in an Islamic school I was teaching in and I believe the student just came back from overseas with his father who was studying Islam. It's important that our children are given a solid well rounded education of who they are.

Many of us came to Islam like myself in our late teens early adulthood and had perceptions and ideas on life already many of which may not have been in line with the teachings of Islam. Unlearning information or ideas again are extremely difficult if possible. It is truly a mercy from Allah to have previously learned ideologies that are astray from His religion to be replaced with the correct ones. I contend though many of the ideologies and perceptions we African Americans hold was taught on what it is to be black or African American and does not even come from our own opinion recollections or research. We define ourselves threw words and deeds. some of the words we use in defining ourselves today should not be given the honor and pride that is attached to them.

WORDS ARE POWERFUL

Savage/Savant

Hustlers/entrepreneurs

Street knowledge/Knowledge of self

Nigga/negus

There's a couple words in particular I'd like to take issue with the 'N"-word is not one of them unfortunately, I must yield my argument on the N word given it IS so much in common usage and accepted in our community, the notion or idea that we have taken the power out of it and the control over it I believe may have been an ideology manipulated by others to us. So stating or believing the N word has become a term of affection but can be still equally used to offend even between two African Americans raises questions on how can it realistically be both, but again I yield any argument I could make cause that would be a whole separate book that would take years of research to make a reasonable argument. Plus, I would need to delete from my vocabulary also unfortunately which again would extremely difficult if possible to do. Words shape and create our reality. One word I want to contest is "Savage",I cant standit that this word isused to give honor to someone. first when we have knowledge of and reflect on the favor our Lord has granted to mankind first by creating and fashioning or shaping us with His two hands, that are not like the hands of any human being. He continued to favor on man by elevating us above other creations. It goes against the honor and favor given to us to now look to gain honor by comparing ourselves to some of the lowest of the other creation from the animals .A true savage animal has no code of conduct they live by. A male savage beast will kill the kids of a female he wants to mate with because they carry the scent of their father. Now, make a comparisons to a man who's jealously or disliking of the children of a women he wants to be with and shows little interest in them or is mean towards them he would be labeled as wrong. What would think or say of a man who commits a savage act like that of the animal I described we could make no excuse or look further into to it for understanding as to why, it would be without question condemned. Im not sure even Hollywood could make a movie based on that plot to be so appealing to individuals with any moral conscious.

Taking a historical look at how this word Savage was used to justify enslaving Africans should also take the pride out of this term being associated to a person character. It was the view of the British colonizers that the Africans they encountered were savages and barbaric. This help justify enslaving and forcing Christianity on them ironically in such a savage and barbaric way, as found in the book "How to make a negro Christian" or the "Negro Christianized, by Cotton Mather (1706)

There is much evidence to prove that many of the early slaves who were brought to America were not Christian when they arrived. A large population of them were Muslim. Along with various tribal beliefs. One of the greatest lies ever told is that Christ, (upon him be peace) was a white man with blonde hair and blue eyes, its implications and the ripple affect it has is unmeasurable, when it is written in their txt he had skin of bronze and wooly type hair meaning he was a man of color with an afro. I know his race is not embedded into the fundamental principals and beliefs of Christianity but was manipulated by the Europeans and used against the Africans to help enslave them. This is another reason why reading was forbidden to slaves it would have been difficult to treat them in such an evil manner then allow them to discover that the one they are being taught to call on as their savior looks just like them

Looking back historically at the geographical location of many of the prophets and messengers the depiction of them as white becomes clear that it is falsely and maliciously told. To be completely clear all of this is the tricks of Shaytan as he vowed to Allah to mislead man in general from the straight path not a particular race as he saytan was the first racist when he claimed to be better than Adam for the difference of their creation after saytan was commanded to prostrate Adam along with other inhabitant of paradise (surah 7verse12) So the plot of saytan will be meticulous and maliciously testing each individual and group of people in ways to keep all of humanity at odds. I remind myself and urge others not to get caught up on black and white issues for it is a trick of the shaytan, also from a worldly view the name of the game has always been chest not checkers so being stuck on racial dominance plays right into the tricks of Satan .Even as I clearly am urging African Americans to raise the level of the playing field and take a stronger vantage point than we have been standing it goes beyond black and white I want us to view it as an obligation of gratitude to our Lord for favouring us to become muslims knowing and worshipping Him correctly . Rabana laka hamd (to my Lord is do the praise) so the fight is against evil in whatever form fashion race or gender it appears to establish good in the earth. Our youth have to be prepared to grab the baton and run their leg of the race taken us to a higher level. This battle or test is truly a marathon not a sprint. This life is transitory and we were advised to live in it as traveler passing through. Our passing through could take 70 years or more with others we leaving behind our children will follow and carry on what we have left behind. So moving forward well informed of who they are requires complete knowledge of our lineage.

We cannot raise them in a bubble so there will be images and perspectives that will influences their reality as to who they are as African Americans, which society will remind them of, and could be detrimental to the vision they have of where they come from and the potential they have to succeed in this world, even as first and foremost they are Muslims and should make this their identity. Even with that being said or the case race will always be a factor rather externally or internal. Allah created us as different tribes and nations so we may identify one another not to despise one another.

One thing I realized talking and researching information to help write this book is that the only or most best known companion of the prophet Muhammad wetalk about is Bilal the first muadhan , who was ironically a slave that was eventually freed .This can perpetuate the idea of Africans being slaves for young African Americans looking at the history of Islam. What is not as well known is one of the descendants of the prophet, may the peace and blessings be upon him, Muhammad Al-Nafs Al-Zakia the son of Abdullah the son of Ali the son of Abu Talib who was a pure blooded Arab from his mom and dad side was described as being black-skinned and huge At tabari is quoted as saying "Muhammad Al-Nafs Al Zakia was tall, jet black-skinned and huge . He was nick named the Bituminous because of his blackness and Abu Jafar Al Mansour use to call him Charcoal .Further more looking at history of our beloved prophet Muhammad (may peace and blessings be upon him)and his struggle to establish Islam across all lands for again he (may peace and blessings be upon him) was sent as a mercy for all of mankind from the sirah(life of) the prophet, may peace and blessings be apon him, was the migration to Abyssinia that the prophet, may peace and blessings be upon him, urged his companions to make hijra to because of the persecution the Muslims received in Mecca and the King in Abyssinia, who was Christian, was just and would not interfere with them practicing Islam. Abyssinia is modern day Ethiopia. There were two migrations from Mecca one to Ethiopia which helped Islam spread and grow in Northern Africa, and consequently east and west Africa also. This was happening during the same period in which some Muslims migrated to Madinah and established a community there. So the role of Africans in the establishment of Islam is more vast than what may be commonly told though alhamdulilah there are books that detail this clearly like"Illuminating The darkness: The virtues of Blacks and Abysinians" byAbu Faraji ibn Jawzi is a good one that comes to mind. I raise this point to say we need to thoroughly examine all the information our youth consume and be certain they have the full picture. As we know growing up people often look to mirror themselves behind individuals found to have characteristics we admire.

One thing I learned in my pusuit of my bachelors in education from Temple University degree is a problem many African American youth have with the literature they read in schools is that they do not see themselves in the readings because they are mainly from a white American perspective and this hinders the connection made to it. Similarly our role in Islam should not be marginalized when taught to our youth and telling others about Islam it leaves room for the argument I've heard from Muslims and non-Muslims alike that much of the practices in Islam are from Arab culture. Not seeing how much we're intimately connected to the establishment of Allah's religion during the time of the prophet Muhammad, peace and blessings be apon him ,and many of the prophets and messengers before him, may peace be upon them all. Yes the aim and focus need to be on learning how to properly worship Allah when reading and studying **Isl**am not about race I am bringing this issue up cause we are a people who don't have AGE old traditions from our culture that we hold onto that have been passed down due to the cut off slavery caused so we keep looking to define ourselves.   Our youth need to be fed all the positive imagery we can give them cause society is surely making the negative so popular and desirable Our youth see the legacy we have in America go from slaves to thugs, killers, bitches and hoes with not enough attention directed to the honor we have before the establishment of these states and after coming out of the physical bondage of slavery. We need to teach them about all the honor in our lineage and to be like those with honorable mention not of the shameless sinful individuals that has reached high status around the world. We should explain and dismantle the thought that we went from slaves to niggas and thugs, thousands of years of blood sweat and tears given to allow them to come to know and serve their Lord in the best way. Our youth should feel indebted to those who came before them and more importantly to Allah so they may create a legacy to help the banner of Islam to raised overall other religions here and around the world.   We have to not just pray for change but put in the work to make it happen.   Education in a wide range of areas is vital to our success.

Education became my major in college switching from business when I took a good assessment of our communal circumstances and where I could have the greatest impact before completing my Bachelors in education I had to my practicum. I taught at a middle school from my old neighborhood. It was very interesting and insightful. A school over 90% African American and I was the only male African American teacher aside from an Art teacher who was only there once a week. I vividly remember an occasion a student was sent to my class because of bad behavior his teacher put him out while talking to him learning his name I could see the resemblance of his parents and I informed the student of how well I knew his parents aunts and uncle he blew it off like it didn't mean anything. When his father brought him back to school as it was required do to his behavior he brought him to my class said in front of the student If you have any more problems out of him dog him and walked away I had the biggest smile on my face I looked at him and said I told you. One of the funniest situations was I had a family member as a student my cousins daughter who was so bothered when I made it none to the other students we were related they picked on her it amused me though. I had another situation where I came to visit my mom and a couple my students were sitting on the steps with my little sister. I harassed them a bit they were so shocked to see me and to learn this whole time their teacher was Godfrey's son you know tiny's lil boy it opened up a line of communication with my students that may not have been available without them being able to make a connection with me outside of school knowing their parents and some knowing mine one kid even lived across the street from my parents. Circumstances arise like this more often where our youth begin to be influenced by and look up to learned and respectable men from the community wanting to follow in their paths as they do the criminals in the criminals the see we can see a change in community that will have such a powerful and positive ripple effect to be felt world wide.

 I reflect on this to point out a great way we can build and have a strong impact on our community through education. Alhamdulilah there are a few Islamic schools in the city we need to work together in securing our children education it will take some maneuvering but there are a number of schools that was closed around the city that could be purchasd and made into a complete school where we could have full control over the curriculum and structure of the school it being a religious institution and not confined to the same curriculum of public school though we would need to cover some secular information though . Have the men teach the boys as the reach a certain age and the girls taught by the woman This is attainable and would have such a great impact on the city. We recognize our spending power pool our resources together and purposely make steps towards creating a sound forward thinking productive community we need to nurture more professionals in our community.

We should be creating financial institutions sending our youths to hajj and umrah yearly as well as programs to visit the people of knowledge building relationships at a young age with communities in other countries.

Stop Looking for reasons to snap

Ostentatious-characterized by vulgar or pretentious display; designed to impress or attract notice

Everything in life was created with its opposite so the only thing that will combat and destroy all the self hate in our community is self love.This will only come from first having complete knowledge of self and he truth is what it and the simplicity of it can at times seem out of touch with reality because it doesn't agreed with opinions just is what it is .we have to reform our way of thinking. This is not just for "Thinking outside the block, in terms of it being strictly an urban mentality because this ideology have traveled beyond urban areas. The mentality of I'm always on go(or going from 0-100 real quick) !!!!!i for the most part is envolving some drama or negativity. We need to rethink our adaptation of such a mentality. I was taught this move out dude mentality put you among the first to get caught up and you wouldn't last long this way .The front line soldiers are there to be sacrificed and make way for more decorated soldiers to come in and get credit for winning the battle.

Take a look at social media and the so called "Reality T.V."and you really see ostentatious defined In the actions of individuals. Decency and Morals are traded off for likes reviews and a check.

Emotions cloud reasoning and this applies to emotions on every range or scale mad, sad joy, love and hate can cloud judgement and have you respond in a manner that you would not have had you with a clear level head thinking through your response to any situation. This is the approach needed to be taken in all our dealings with family and friends alike the "irking" campaign has been running too long in our community its not just a term used, words are powerful and this mentality has been spoken into existence in how we view and deal with one another adding to the short tolerance 0-100 .This view is self-hate take a second to consider your own short comings and faults that should give way to understanding others circumstances, and short coming. This is not to suggest that you accept whatever attitude may come from people but there is a reasonable way to deal with it. We need to restore genuine love and concern for each other to create the environment desired to raise our children so they can go out and better the world we live in. I am passionate about the idea that when we indigenous people from the continent of Africa standup be recognized for who we truly are the world will yield and follow us in good. It is the nature of our people. Allah has chosen our Ancestral lineage to carry His message to mankind for ages. This fact has been lied about ,covered up, and distorted but this truth must be identified and reintroduced to our youth to give them right identification of who they really are washing away this criminal identification that pleagues our community, propagated to our children. We are descendants of prophets , messengers, Kings and men of Honor that goes far beyond the establishment of this land called America we know today. A statement that comes to mind describing the mindset of too many African Americans from Cater g Woodsoon born 12-19-1875 died04-1950 who was an American Historian, author ,journalist and founder of Association for African American Life and history. Mr. Woodson was one of the first scholars to study history of African diaspora (the world-wide collection of communities descended from native Sub-Saharan Africa predominantly in Americas) where he states

"If you can make a man think he is justly an outcast, you do not have to order him to back door. He will go without being told; and if there is no back door, his very nature will demand one."

-Carter G. Woodson

Ahmad Abdullah

Chapter 20/20 vision well 2021 vision

Husbandry-The care , cultivation and breeding of crops and animals ;the scientific control and management of a branch farming and especially of domestic animals; the control or judicious use of resources; conservation of domestic animals.

This financial market may seem far fetched for most of us living in the northern united states especially urban areas but it is available to us also. Pennsylvania is a farm state like New Jersey. My interest grew when I was delivering Hello Fresh foods in southern New Jersey' as I was driving from one home to home in different township I noticed the large area of corn fields and one day made me google different uses of corn cause all that corn could not be for supermarkets and human consumption. I knew Corn goes in the feed for horses , chickens and other farm animal but it had to be more to it than that I learned corn was used in ethanol, and bio based plastics. I can see now why the corn fields are so plentiful there it may even be encourage by city or state officials to grow corn to make the state a leader in that industry. Husbandry ismore interesting to me do to me because I already have a love for horses and animals all together, and agriculture. Horses are like a family business. My uncle has exposed and raised all of my family and even our friends on handling horses not just how to ride but care for also. My uncle is well known in Philadelphia and surrounding areas for his work with horses which has been all my life im 46 he is now 80 and still actively involved .He has been in the papers on the news honored at the Barnes center in philadelphia for his work in the community introducing inner city youth to horses as a means of keeping them out of trouble .His influence on me is so that I **transformed** my car garage at my home into a barn holding two ponies and two horses that belong to him in which I became caretaker for them feeding cleaning them and the stalls letting out to stretch their legs daily. This along with a the advise from the Prophet Muhammad to fathers and their duty to their sons to teach them stating we should teach them swimming, horse back riding and archery, this hadith is found in At-tirmithi .It led me to create a summer program where these things are taught along with gardening of course we played sports but it was baseball and soccer. The playground where I took the children had soccer instructors and they allotted two days out the week at designated times for my children to learn soccer, which by the way is the most popular sport in the world.

On to my 20/20vision intend to form a landscaping crew out of the older children who are or have attended my camp from the first year in 2017 as a foundation for them to generate income to form other business one day we were in front of the Ranch which is the name of the camp a tree cutter who I would get to drop his tree shavings off so I could show the youth how to make mulch something the tree cutter didn't even know cause he said a company to allow him to dump the shavings who probably then turned around and sold them to a company that sold mulch, well as the guy say the children planting the bushes he came over to tell the children passionately telling how good of a skill and trade they were learning, he went on totell them he knows a guy who started in the landscaping business when he was 15 and abot to retire now in his early fifties after making millions and still has some profitable contracts that he sub out making money from home this man's motto is "I make green off green" and think for a minute grass is not going nowhere homes and businesses with it has to keep up the maintenance of it or will be fined. Businesses like malls hotels, hospitals need landscaping for the appearance sake not just about a fine this is a very profitable business and not just a summer time thing it can go 9 months out the year at least and in that time done right can accumulate enough income to help create another source of income to create jobs for others. Really teach or mentor them on how to build their own community and economy. I am looking now for a small farm or ranch right outside the city where I could have a bigger program working with a larger number of children. I would provide a van service to transport the children to and from designated meeting spot or spots. The vision I have for this one excites me, makes some nights restless, when I envision all that could be accomplished when I get this together insha Allah.

Back to the youth I would like to mentor them on how to create an economic base to help stabilize our community. I will select a few who I've seen display the attitudes and characteristics needed for such an endeavour. Also shows intrest in outdoor work I have one in mind who is going to attend Saul high school which is an agriculturally based school in Philadelphia to come and help with the mentoring of the campers sharing what he learned in school. It was great we had an opportunity to take the campers by Saul just the summerof 2019 to spend a day the interacting with the animals and getting a since of what it is to be a farmer. Again I know this idea seems far fetch from a brother up north and from north philly but im driven to do this for a number of reasons not all economic, religiously it can benefit our youth to reflect on the beauty of Allah creates everything along with the the favor and trust He placed on mankind that he favored us above all other creation subjecting some to us as beast of burden along with those we eat.

I reflect on the days of Eid al-adha when it is the responsibility of the Muslims to slaughter. Looking at the number of people who participate in this act of worship made mein 2019 while at the farm sit back and try estimate how much owners of the farms or slaughter houses we go to gross in the three days in which we are to slaughter. An easy six figures can be grossed in three days from my calculations I think about this and say I've invested a lot of money in different businesses over the years now "Thinking outside the block' this is one I definitely must venture into insha Allah for both financial and religious benefits Im sure there are many of us especially from up North who may look down on farming as some old slave work. Ironicaly enough as I qoated from W E B dubouis who debated with Booker T Washington over the direction the newly freed slaves should take to build an economical foundation. Dubious differed with Mr. Wahington who felt we should stay in the labor field to generate money to help build independence but now as owners not just indigenous workers. Dubouis was a savant studied and taught at Harvard as well as other prestigious universities felt education was the key and they were both correct, and we should inquire and venture into this field of agriculture not just for the economic prosperity but health reasons as well it is no secret that animals are being shot with hormones and who knows what else that we then consume even our fruits and vegetables are not safe. They are sprayed with chemicals that can cause illnesses we dont even know. Recently I have been talking to my son and encouraging him about being a veterinarian which could serve him well financially and help out the community as he could learn and inform of the harm in the meats we eat. Even some meats labelled halal need to questioned. Working in the food industry I've seen cases of chicken labeled halal that were as big as the ones not labeled chickens don't get but so big on their own, another reason we need to do this is because every year for eid al adha we go to farms to slaughter we mention Allah's name over the animal when we slaughter but have no guarantee that they were raised and feed in a halal manner we must take better care and responsibility for these matters. There have been in recent years so many cases of young people men and women with cancer and other illnesses that could be related to the food an even the water we drink. We should have individuals in these fields of study to help inform us of the dangers that exist. How to stay away from them also. With further reflection on the before mentioned lecture given by daud Adib from gemantown to muslim town I ask myself given the opportunity to have a section of the city or a town like quakertown or what occurred in Hamtramack, Michigan which is said to be first Muslim city in council in the U.S., would we make it off the porch before differing spoiled the opportunity. Would lobbying for positions of authority would stall us coming out the gate. Would this town even be desirable to live in. Could we come together under the banner of Islam with the common goal of establishing Allah's religion in the land or will Ego's(eliminating god out) hinder or handicap our efforts. I am an optimist so I firmly believe we can achieve such a goal. Firs we must hold ourselves to higher standards. Raise the bar on ourselves!!!!!!!!!!!come on now people lets come from under neath this syndrome of Willy Lynch which was set allegedly set in motion and intended to last for 300 years dating back to the year 1712, which by my calculation should have expired in 2012. I cannot rest and settle for the idea that we are under some spell , so predictable or easily manipulated as a people for in our lineage are men of wisdom and great thinkers that lived over the last 300 years. We need to build off of the works of those who have committed to the development and advance of our people corrected with adhering to the Qur'an and Sunnah of our beloved prophet Muhammad(), success is imminent.

Thinking outside the Border

We native people from the continent of Africa who were taken by force then brought to America are the only race or nationality that has no connection with its homeland in this land of immigrants. This needs to change to help create that balance the world need a movement should take place where Africans are embraced in this country from amongst the indigenous people of Africa in greater fashion than we embrace other foreign nationalities. In our communities here we support the businesses and revere the practices of Asian/chines, Cuban ,Dominican or Hispanics who come to our communities open businesses to support their families here and back in their home lands, but will not sit amongst these African owned businesses to get a since of what real African culture is like and build a relationship with them that could reach back to Africa . When I operated my café in Philadelphia there was a car wash around the corner that was owned and operated by a brother from Mali I began to establish a rapport with the guy who ran the place he was making arraignments for to meet up with some of his family members there told me all I would need was to pay for my flight there and everything else would be handled by his family when I got there housing travel and food accommodation all would be handled by them. I made arraignments for the flight something came up I had to cancel my trip then had some issues with my health but insha Allah by end of 20/20(now20/21due to covid) I was planning to visit west Africa a couple countries in the region I was extended the same offer from a friend who lives in Ghana like the one from Mali another place I'd like to visit especially given its place in this history of African slave trade there are museums and artifacts there that tell the stories of some the first slaves to be captured held to be brought to America and the others to follow them .The world has been put on quarantine in March of 20/20 so my trip will have to wait insha Allah till end of 20/21 insha Allah West Africa is where many of the slaves who were brought by the Europeans to America were originally from there is a similar place in Jamaica of slave qaurters, which was one of the middle passages, I seen the remnance of when I visited the island.

Acckee and salt fish is a national dish in Jamaica that is revered not only for its great taste but its place in rebellion by the Africans held there .The Africans superior knowledge of agriculture, which played a large part of why they were brought to America in hopes to have the land cultivated by them. The Africans knew ackee which is a fruit native to west Africa , if picked and ate before it is ripe could be deadly. So the African slaves would serve it to the Europeans before it was ripe to kill them and try to free themselves from bondage though they could not make it back home. The native Africans were built to live off the land and built civilizations wherever they settled down at. Which is how we have these beautiful islands today like Jamaica, Trinidad and Tobago and other Carribean islands in the region that were also middle passages in slave trafficking, which includes Puerto Rico , Dominican Republic and Cuba , the citizens there have the same origins as we indigenous people from the continent of Africa living in America. A relationship could be built there too along with African nations not just from the western part either. This appeal being made for the people of color here in America, particularly the Muslims a to rise up from mental slavery living up to or better yet live down to the negative perceptions of us making them realities, extends to those islands and islanders as well. Many of the ideologies actions modes of thinking and lack of morals, dignity and high standards displayed are not historically original characteristics of people whose origins are from Africa so a reconnection is of extreme importance to progress and moving in the direction of prosperity and honor that is historically in line with descendants of Africa. Let this appeal to colored citizens of America and other nations to make a conscious effort to get to know individuals from Africa in an attempt to get to know Africa to better know ourselves, Yield best you can some of our perceptions on Africa and Africans that were maliciously tainted to keep this connection severed. There's not only strength in numbers but the potential quality as well as quantity of people that would come from this connection is alarming to others outside of our race ,which should make it more desirable from us looking forward with a world view of progress. Humility would need to be practiced on all ends with the goal being a global achievement and long-term relationship. Now I'm not encouraging we have to go to the extent of Marcus Garvey's view of all us leaving and moving to Africa though I wouldn't discourage it either We could us America as a means of income and global influence. If more of us would visit Africa often this would come about anyway after seeing the truth about the people, the land and the opportunities there.

Black lives matter

In 2013 in response to the death /murder of Travon Martin Alicia Garz, Patrisse Cullors and Opal Tometi started the movement to affect the political and social view for people of color. The movement has become a platform on which many of the social and systematic injustice towards people of color is argued from. We have seen in recent time the move rise to a global level of recognition and used as a platform all around the world against injustice. It has taken such a place in society and history now it can be found painted on the street in front of this nations capital. All over sports arenas throughout this nation. The Negro basketball associations players backed it by wearing jersey's with it on back instead of their names along with the names of people who gained national attention for the injustice acted out towards them along with slogans that signify their cruel treatment like "I Can't breath symbolizing Eric Garners last words to NYC police officer who placed him in an illegal choke hold back in 2014.The movement

My one issue with this movement is that in the year 2020 we are still asking to be relevant or of importance to a system and nation that from its birth has stated clearly its views and position on the lives of people of color. It is our obligation and duty to each other to share the sentiments and consideration amongst each other that the movement is seeking from the American justice system. if we don't seem to matter to each other how can we truly expect it from a system or other races or a system that thrives off our ill treatment of each other Black on Black crime happens at a more alarming rate than any other crime committed against us. It should be safe to assume that the system should be just to all citizens but since the birth of this nation it has proven that people of color are not going to be treated justly. We weren't included in the constitution under the statement "We the people " because at that time we weren't considered people only property.

An in-depth look into our role in the establishment of America and the world for that matter how we have pioneered the development of this nation economically culturally and beyond should bring us to a point where we no longer need recognition from anyone. This self-recognition will create the reality we seek for the system to identify us with.

Look at this relationship we have with the American justice system like a woman(people of color)who has been in a long term relationship with a man(American justice system)for far too long and she has never been treated to the level of her worth because the man is too arrogant to and wont give the proper consideration though it's clear how she has made him better than what he could have ever been without her. This relationship has even taken her to the point where she almost completely forgot her value she almost forgot that without the contributions she made to his current existence his status would be average, at best. It will not be until she had enough of being mistreated and undervalued take a stands within herself that being alone and just moving on would be better than staying under the current circumstances that at shell find herself again and move forward head held high knowing he couldn't do better but she can all on her own.

From this similitude I I wana make it clear that leaving the tragic relationship with American justice system don't necessarily mean everyone pick up and leave that's not reasonable we all cant go.Hijrah (migration) from America is a topic amongst the Muslim here in is talks of making hijra to a country that lives by the Sharia'ah.

There are African countries that live under Sharia'ah law though most times when this conversation is had its regarding an Arab nation to make hijrah to. Again, we all can't leave, in all actuality we all don't want to either. What we can do is form an alliance with each other from state to state start building our own economy. This will be the clearest way to show how much we matter in America. It is no secret how strong the spending power from people of color, you take that along with the revenue from our culture regarding sports and entertainment pool all these resources operate as society within this society the magnitude of how much we matter would blind this America from how bright we would shine making it hard to find its wat without us. Like a man who after being without his better half for a short period of time will try to fill that void in his life by either luring back the best women he's ever had or seek to replace her with another.

BLACK IS NOT A RACE

Black is not a race which means consequently neither is white there is no scientific bases on which we label a group of people a color this is social-economical basis that has been indoctrinated into our society so much so it is not only accepted here to identify /divide people but worldwide as well. Before this social economical distinction for groups of people the identification was made by tribes or cultural location, In 1730 in the nations first national census the population was not only counted it was racially classified this classification impacted policies the country formed.

In North America thousand of years before Columbous landed his ships in the Bahamas a different groups of people visited and inhabited America its estimated that more than 12,000 years before Europeans arrived in the 15th century millions of people were living in North America when the Europeans arrived. Some nomadic tribes traveled through Asia over the Baringia which is now the Baring strait. Into Alaska heading south and east many of them of African origin. There was travel to and from America by Africans before the 15th century with the European invasion. The story written by the Europeans into the history books is not only incomplete but inaccurate or to speak candidly a Bunch of Lies that have become the foundation upon which many ideologies , beliefs, laws and the like have been formed. Folks look deeper into race in America and the world uncover some of the lies that were written come to your own conclusion on race relationships by forming a relationship with individuals from other races. Limit best you can outside influence and opinions when concluding and forming your position on race relations . This country has an agenda for keeping us racially divided that I would encourage us all not to stay deceived by. To my people of color I urge us to make our whole thing to restore ourselves to the rightful place in the world as leaders and not to make our whole agenda be to confront or defeat the plot of the "White man", which is actually a system created hundreds of years ago. Yes it still favors one over others groups of people in America but the objective needs to aimed at learning the laws of the system in order to work with in them making them work in our favor it is possible. I reiterate my point it should start with creating our own economy, building a relationship with African nations, holding ourselves accountable for ill-mannered behaviors and conduct not befitting of a leader .Raise the bar on ourselves and Reach it!!!

What's Your whole thing?!!!!

This is a question from a good friend and I would ask someone being facetious when we weren't feeling the conversation of an individual talking in our presence, this question now I pose to myself and others to ponder over reflect on and respond to with action. What is my whole thing? I am sharing with you now in my writing I urge all who read or hear about this book to answer this question for yourself write it down revisit as often as needed to confirm for yourself that you are staying true to your words with the actions you do daily. Correct yourself as needed to be part of the solution not part of the problem just as the saying goes if you are not part of the so lution you are part of the problem. I ask, are you aiming just to make a dollar or to make a difference which is totally fine if that's your whole that's you're thang. Question, Will you let your ego hold you hostage or will you allow yourself to be a host to the Al mighty and His will? Sharing mercy, kindness and goodness with all those you come into contact with regardless of their race, religion, ethnic background, geographical location, and even treatment of you. Love will win over hate. It starts with a love for the Creator, yourself, those closes to you and who you have a responsibility over What's your whole Thing? Have you defined it or have you consciously or unconsciously.

Ahmad Abdullah

STROKE

This has to seem so off topic from rest of the book but stay with me I wanna make an analogy between the state of African American and the affects a stroke has on an individual.

Let me begin by first stating I experienced a stroke myself in 2018 and still today working towards recovery. I have typed this with one hand due to the paralasys on my left side. Writing is part of my therapy helps to keep brain active take a break from the physical therapy this is in part like speech therapy I used to go to which I saw as cognitive therapy from the skills they tested .A stroke could affect a person speech this was not the case for me but I know a brother who had to relearn the alphabet after his stroke. Everybody's stroke is different the affect on the body and mind will vary for each individual so will the recovery .One thing that is the same for any one who experience a stroke is the mercy of Allah is needed to make any progress in recovery. Patience, perseverance and prayer is a must.

Analogy

As a result of a stroke paralasis t one side of the body occurs. This causes a lack of blood circulation to the brain and affected side .For the purpose of this anology I want the blood circulation to be represented as love in our community which has been paralised .it still exist but with limited mobility. The brain in this analogy is the continent of Africa with all the knowledge it holds of life in general the blueprint to much of what we have and know today of science, medicine, agriculture, construction, religion and more can be traced back to the place of our ancestors.

A terminology used in describing recovery from stroke is muscle memory. I'd like to define our recovery as moral memory. Muscles have a memory from prior movement before stroke. We indigenous people from the continent of Africa don not have first-hand knowledge of what life on the continent of Africa was like to restore ourselves to it without the need of in-depth research on the true nature and history of African people, which would need to include a relationship with present day citizens of Africa and the land itself also.

Regarding our moral compass that navigates how we treat one another the memory of this will connection will ignite an energy and life for that will illuminate so bright and serve as a light to the rest of the world to follow. From educating ourselves on true African culture part of which will come from building a relationship with Africa. I'm not nieve to think are no undesirable characteristics to be found on the Largest continent on the planet but I am hopeful we can find more genuinely loving and caring character that will elicit similar character in us to come to the forefront. These immoral acts that we conduct, boast and brag about are not genuinely characteristics from people who's origin from the continent of Africa

The mind is a terrible thing to waste. We are wasting the opportunity to connect to the brain which is Africa.

Interactive Reading

WORDS ARE POWERFUL

Savage/Savant

Hustlers/entrepreneurs

Street knowledge/Knowledge of self

Nigga/negus

    Below replace some words yourself that could help reshape your perception or others our words have power lets lose the idea that we should invite people to hate on us the evil eye is real. This mode of thinking has been spread for too long in our community far even before it has been made popular in the media. take control of the narrative that is being about our existence. How do we want history to remember and record us.

Thinking Outside The Block

More Inter active reading

You the now become the writer- this where you answer
the question for yourself What's your whole thing?

_____
_____
_____
_____
_____
_____
_____
_____
_____
_____
_____
_____
_____
_____
_____
_____
_____
_____
_____
_____
_____
_____
_____
_____
_____
_____
_____

Ahmad Abdullah

So what's your whole thing?

So what's your whole thing?

"To be African American is to be African without any memory and American without any privilege." — James Baldwin

Messenger of Allah said: "The nations are about to call each other and set upon you, just as diners set upon food." It was said: "Will it be because of our small number that day?" He said:

"Rather, on that day you will be many, but you will be like foam, like the foam on the river. And Allah will remove the fear of you from the hearts of your enemies and will throw wahn (weakness) number that day?" He said:

"Rather, on that day you will be many, but you will be like foam, like the foam on the river. And Allah will remove the fear of you from the hearts of your enemies and will throw wahn (weakness) into your hearts." Someone said: "O Messenger of Allah! What is wahn?" He said: "Love of the world and the hatred for death." Sahih: Related by Abu Dawud (no. 4297), Ibn 'Asakirin in Tarikh Dimashq (2/97/8) and others. It

CPSIA information can be obtained
at www.ICGtesting.com
Printed in the USA
BVHW032157230221
600893BV00009B/826